thank you TO BRADLEY UNIVERSITY'S department of communication FOR SUPPORTING THIS PROJECT

ISBN: 978-1-4951-9890-8

Just my Type of Lettering: An Inspirational Guide to Hand Lettering by Chelsie Tamms
Copyright © 2016 by Chelsie Tamms

This book is dedicated in loving memory of my grandmother, who never failed to encourage me to apply myself, "get those good grades" and do what I most enjoy.

I would not be where I am today without the support of my family and friends. I cannot thank my **parents** and **grandparents** enough for their encouragement throughout school, my closest co-workers, **Ham Paredes** and **Alex Mariscal**, for their mentorship and genuine friendship, and my high school art teacher, **Wendy Guss**, for pushing me to pursue my interests from the beginning.

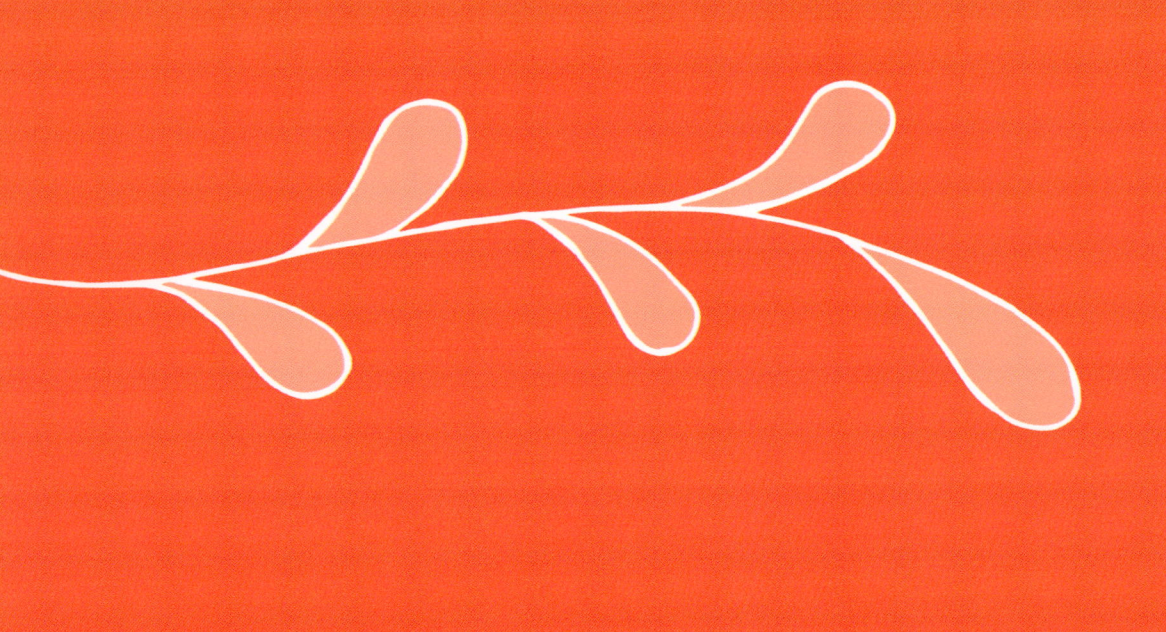

TABLE OF CONTENTS

Introduction................................... **11**
Lettering Tools............................. **14**
Creative Process......................... **16**
How to Vectorize Lettering........ **18**
Developing a Personal Style....... **22**
Projects & Process:
Card Designs.. **24**
Personalized Product Design.......... **26**
Travel Lettering.................................. **28**
Parks & Rec Lettering...................... **30**
Miscellaneous..................................... **32**
Design Inspiration............................. **34**
Hand-Lettered ABC's....................... **38**
Resources...................................... **40**
Project Ideas............................... **41**

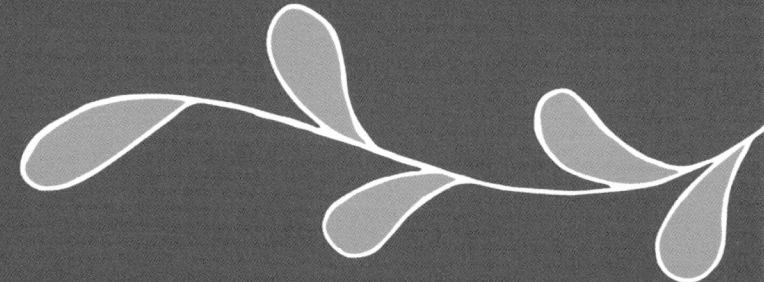

INTRODUCTION

The earliest memory of writing I have is from first grade when the teacher told me I had the best handwriting in the class. Throughout grade school, I remember I often stopped mid-assignment to determine my favorite letter or got distracted on my math homework by how precisely I wrote each number. Because the private school I attended focused more on academics than art, my childhood was filled with art classes primarily after school and throughout the summer months. The greatest lesson I learned in my nine years of private grade school was, "if you don't have time to do it right, you must have time to do it over." It might have been printed on a poster in the classroom or simply lectured endlessly, but it really stuck with me; ultimately forming my detail-oriented and perfectionist mind set — an essential attribute of designers and hand-lettering artists.

The end of eighth grade came with an event that still continues to impact my life. I remember November 14, 2007 and the 11.5-hour spinal fusion surgery to correct my 60-degree curve caused by scoliosis like it was yesterday. It not only left me with two titanium rods and 19 screws running down my spine, but with an amplified drive for pursuing my dreams as an artist. I took 13 art classes throughout my four years at Cary-Grove High School. I fell in love with advertising and design after my first graphic design course and a field trip to Leo Burnett in downtown Chicago. The compositions, posters, t-shirts, and other designs I produced heavily relied on my lettering. My high school art teacher encouraged me to further develop and refine this hand-lettered style, which resulted in my ultimate submission of the first all-design AP 2D design portfolio submitted from my school.

While I was confident in my decision to pursue graphic design as a career, I decided to attend Bradley University for an opportunity to pursue my interests in both Spanish and marketing alongside design. Throughout my college career, my mantra has been: take advantage of every opportunity possible. During college, I became involved in fifteen on-campus organizations, attended more than ten conferences, held eight internships and career-related jobs, and spent five months abroad in Granada, Spain.

Throughout all of these experiences, I built many skillsets and learned an incredible amount about myself — and with this book, I hope to share a little bit of it with all of you.

One of the most influential pieces of advice I received came from a reviewer at a Chicago AIGA Mentor Program portfolio review. At the time, I was struggling to diversify my design portfolio, to which he told me, "do what you love until you can't anymore." His comment further fueled my passion for pursuing my love of hand lettering with all of my heart and energy. I plan to pursue my love of lettering until I can't anymore and I aim to turn it into my full-time career.

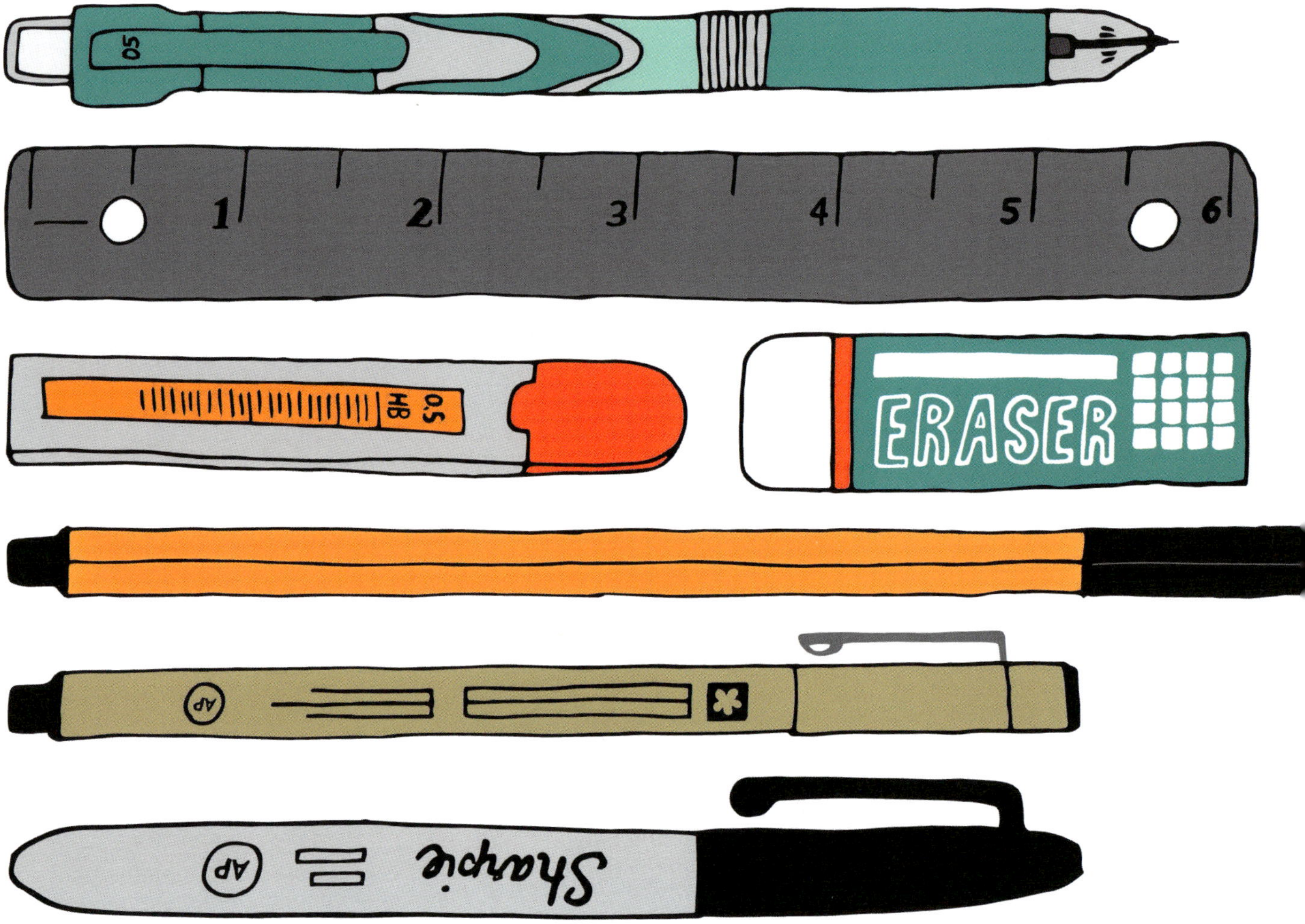

LETTERING TOOLS

Preferences on lettering tools vary by artist, but most are reasonably priced. You can start with tools as simple as pencils, pens, and markers and advance to experimenting with fancier and more expensive tools such as specialty markers, brushes, inks, and paints.

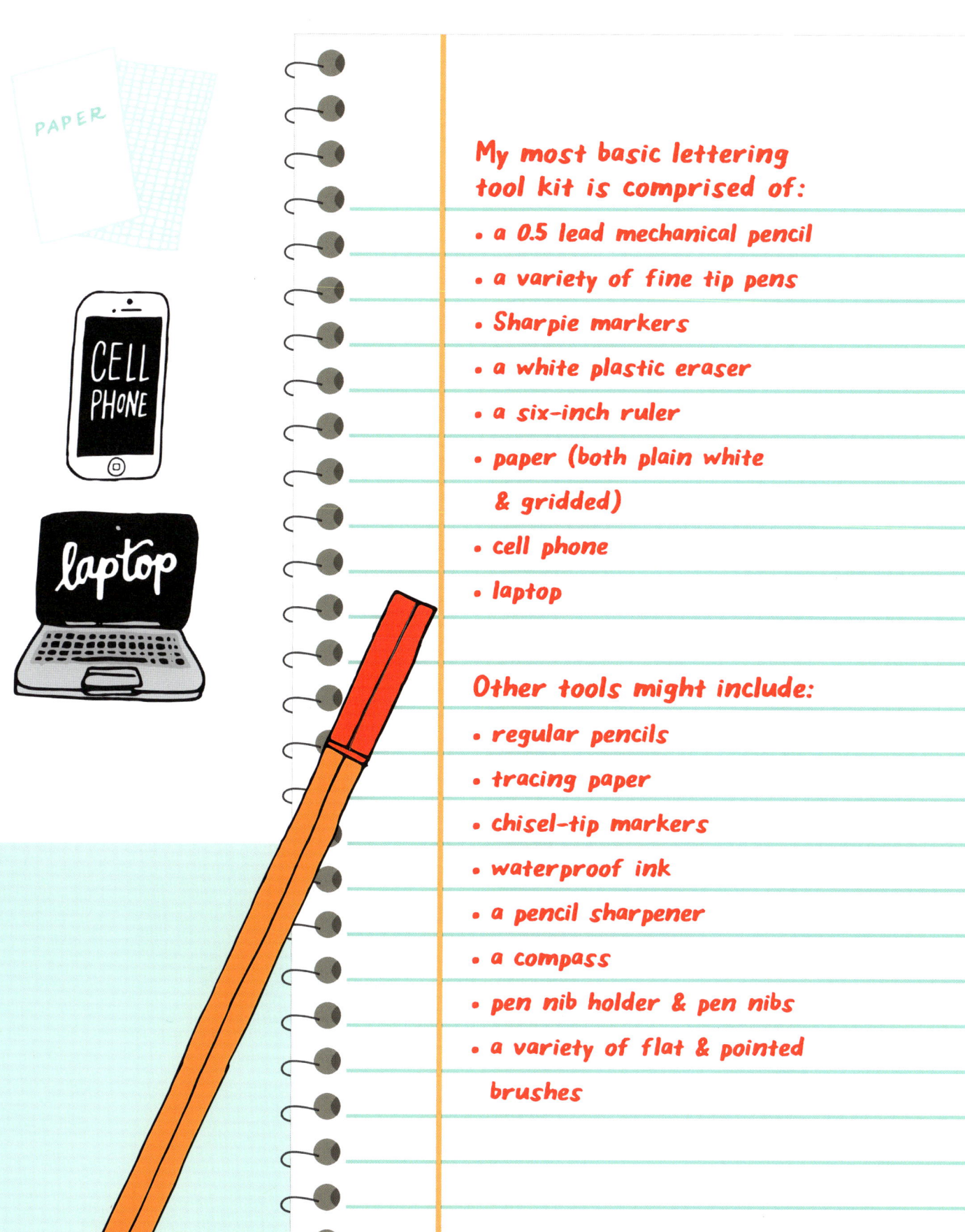

My most basic lettering tool kit is comprised of:

- a 0.5 lead mechanical pencil
- a variety of fine tip pens
- Sharpie markers
- a white plastic eraser
- a six-inch ruler
- paper (both plain white & gridded)
- cell phone
- laptop

Other tools might include:

- regular pencils
- tracing paper
- chisel-tip markers
- waterproof ink
- a pencil sharpener
- a compass
- pen nib holder & pen nibs
- a variety of flat & pointed brushes

the CREATIVE

STEP ONE: RESEARCH, brainstorming & MOOD BOARDS

STEP TWO: thumbnails AND SKETCHING

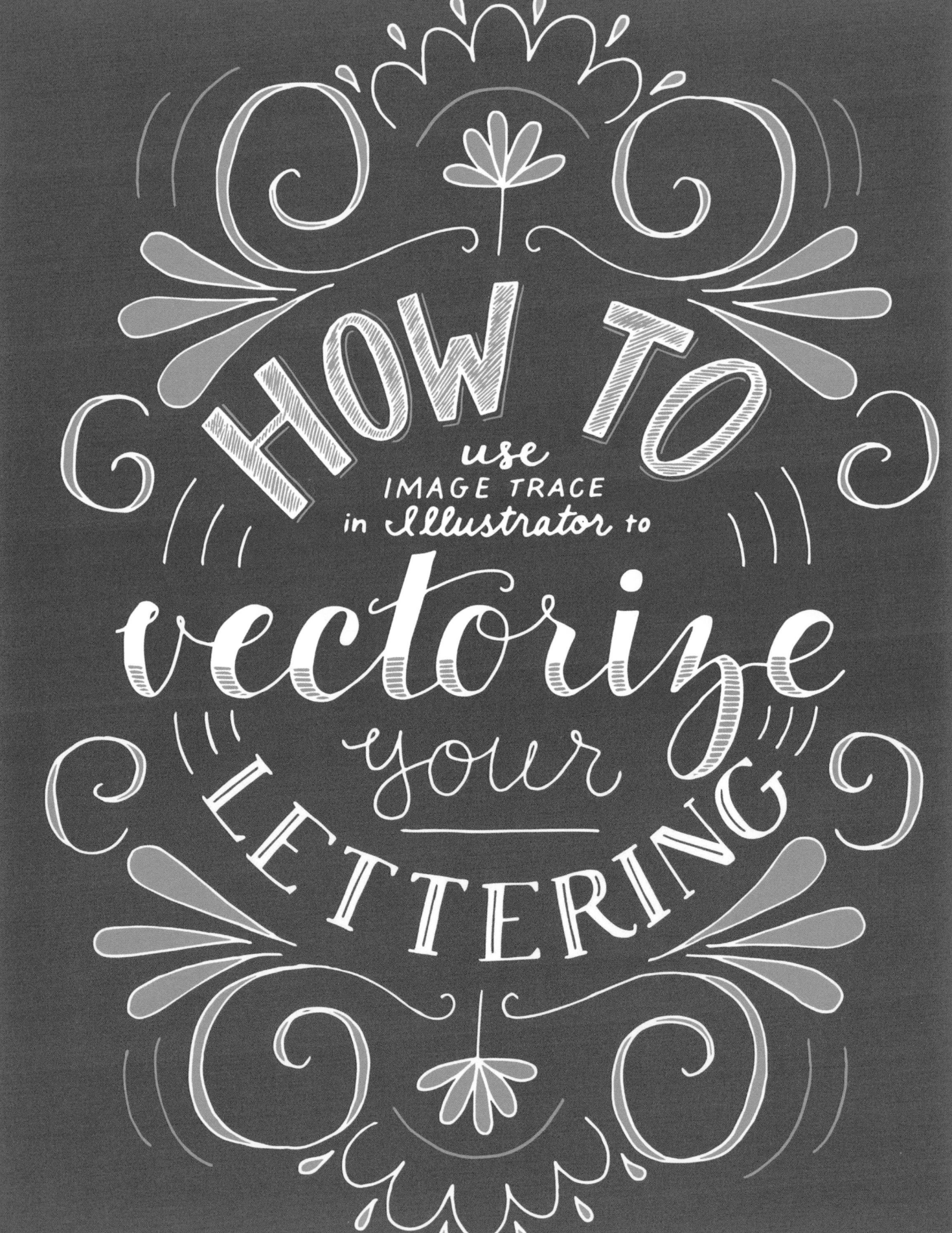

Pencil drawing

Pencil and pen drawing

Pen drawing (with pencil erased)

Scanned image (at 600dpi)

Step 1: Complete drawing
- With high contrast, usually pens/ink

Step 2: Scan
- Optional: edit in Photoshop to ensure high contrast

filled in top of "pencil"

smoothed shapes with eraser tool

adjusted kerning (letter spacing) of "drawing"

Image Trace Result

centered "to" between lines

grouped inline stroke and changed to background color

filled in "vector"

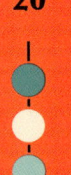

Step 3: Open file in Illustrator and open the tool "Image Trace."
• After pulling up the full toolbar for this tool, you will be able to manipulate the threshold and other advanced settings including paths, corners, and noise to achieve your desired look. If you check the "Preview" box, you can easily determine the effects of your changes before applying them.
• Click "Trace" to apply your changes to the image. You can either select "Ignore White" in the Image Trace settings dialog box or click "Expand" and then use the magic wand tool to eliminate the white.

Step 4: Align elements.
• You can easily "Ungroup" the elements in your scanned image and realign them, manipulate them with the Smooth Tool, Pencil Tool, and Eraser Tool until you get the look and layout that you are going for.

Step 5: Add Color.
• Using the "Paint Bucket" Tool, you can easily fill in different colors throughout your artwork. You can also use the "Shape Builder" tool to fill in lettering you might have left outlined in the initial pen drawing. These tools can save both time and pen ink if you are working towards a solid filled in design. This process also works great if you plan to have a solid letter but would like to have other details that you can draw on the original, because you can easily change the colors of the artwork during this step.

• You can continue to manipulate colors, layout, and variations of your hand-lettered designs until you get what you are looking for. The easiest way to manipulate your color combinations is through the "Edit Colors" feature, which allows you to recolor any given color with a simple click.

Tip: If you struggle with coming up with color combinations, start with grayscale and then utilize the "Edit > Edit Colors" feature to recolor artwork quickly and effortlessly.

TIPS

Get inspired! Find what you like and try to recreate it. Pay attention to how your work differs from the original and embrace the little nuances that make your lettering unique.

Practice! Practice as much as you can and your style will start emerging.

Challenge yourself! Take out a blank sheet of paper and start creating. Allow yourself to letter something that comes completely from your own mind instead of copying a preexisting design.

Tip: Start simple. Try not to overcomplicate your lettering compositions, and instead start out with simple words or phrases. Focus on the way a word can convey its meaning visually.

CARD DESIGNS

This project started as a personal challenge to create a new hand-lettered card design in my sketchbook each day throughout one June. Personal projects are the best way to determine your true interests and passions and to create unique work that helps define your style and refine your skills. I focused on creating a variety of designs, incorporating different styles and sentiments, without being concerned about everything perfectly going together. Choosing sentiments are often a large obstacle to starting a project; this project provided an opportunity to start simple and get basic practice in lettering styles and composition.

PERSONALIZED PRODUCT DESIGNS

The first three weeks of my internship with Custom Personalization Solutions were spent sketching, illustrating, and vectorizing a variety of words, phrases, and quotes for use on a variety of personalized products. Personalized Planet, one of the four companies owned by Custom Personalization Solutions, applied my hand-lettered designs to a variety of products in different product categories. I created a library of hand-lettered artwork and illustrations that the company is able to pull from even long after my internship ended.

Tip: Begin with the future in mind. Organize your files and create templates for designs from the beginning so you can easily access and reuse designs later on.

Tip: Staying creative is important, even when your focus at the time is not solely to produce designs or creative work. Allow yourself time to record and build materials that you can later dig up to create projects.

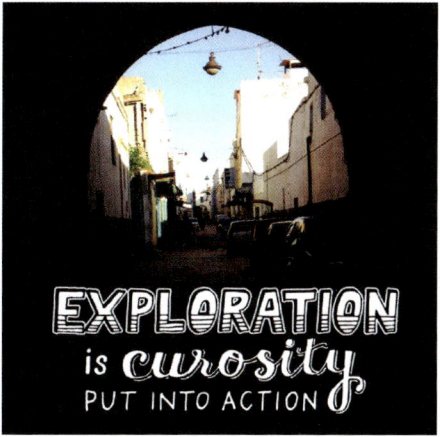

TRAVEL LETTERING

When all of life is going on around you, it can be difficult to stay inspired, motivated, and constantly creating. It is very important to keep practicing. Consistent practice can be very beneficial to allow your situations and surroundings to inspire your work. I spent five months in Granada, Spain studying Spanish and used this time traveling in Europe to work on additional skills like photography. I was also able to document some of my experiences through overlaying applicable hand-lettered quotes over my photographs.

PARKS AND REC LETTERING

Similar to taking inspiration from my travels abroad, I took inspiration from the NBC TV show *Parks and Recreation* in order to develop my next personal project. Finding something you love outside of design and using lettering as a way to illustrate your interests can become a great conversation starter and show others a little more about your personality than other projects you might complete. Personal projects like this one allow you to take total creative freedom and have fun with content that you are truly interested in.

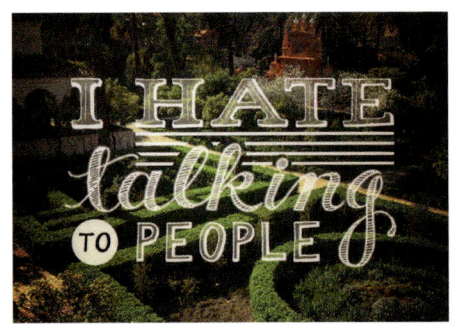

Tip: Pair your interest in developing your lettering skills with something else you are passionate about. It helps make the practice fun and can be a great way to get your work noticed. If you are struggling with ideas, ask around! Chances are some of your friends and family are interested in the same things as you are!

KENMORE CAMPAIGN

Objective: Brainstorm, concept, and develop a branded Kenmore campaign that utilizes a hand-lettered style/aesthetic.

Client: Aisle Rocket Studios/Kenmore

1. Floor Graphic
2. Online Hub Page
3. Step Up Graphic

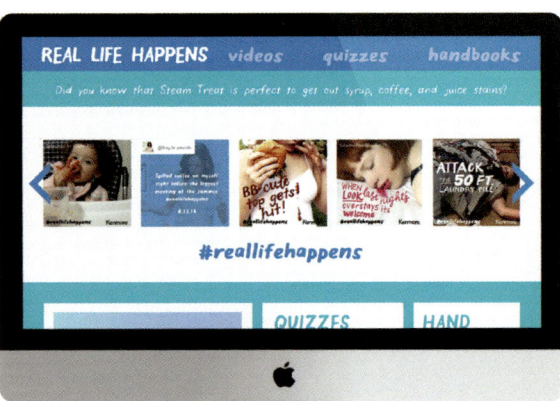

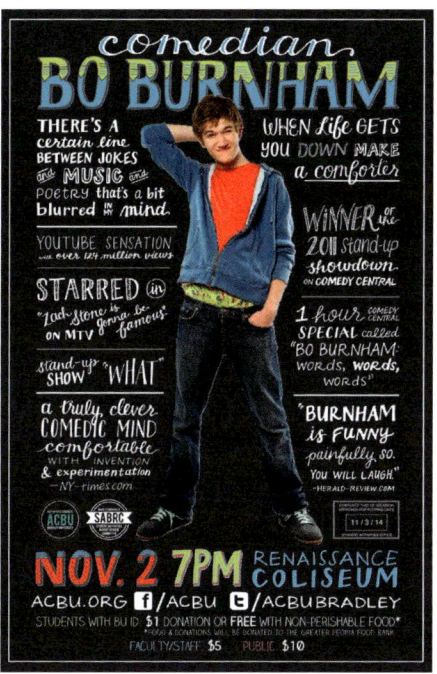

MISCELLANEOUS

PARENTS DAY LETTERING

Objective: Create a custom hand-lettered/illustrated quote designed for Blu Sky Creative as a social media post for Parents' Day.

Client: Blu Sky Creative

BO BURNHAM POSTER

Objective: Create an eye-catching and informative poster to advertise popular comedian Bo Burnham coming to Bradley University's campus.

Client: Activities Council at Bradley University

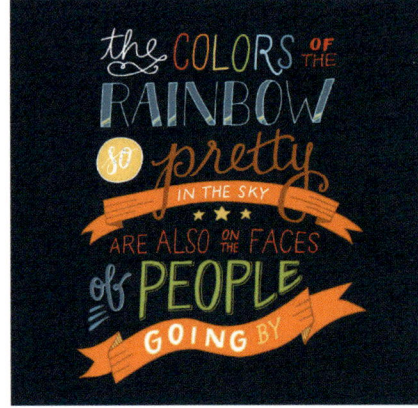

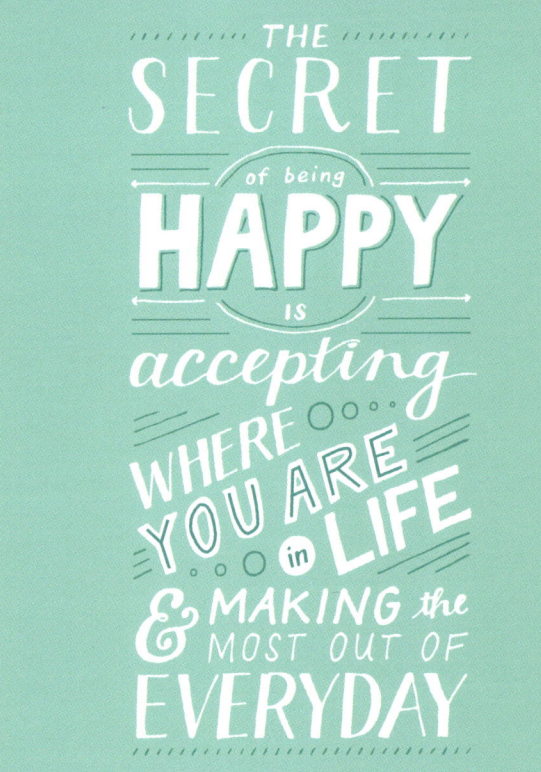

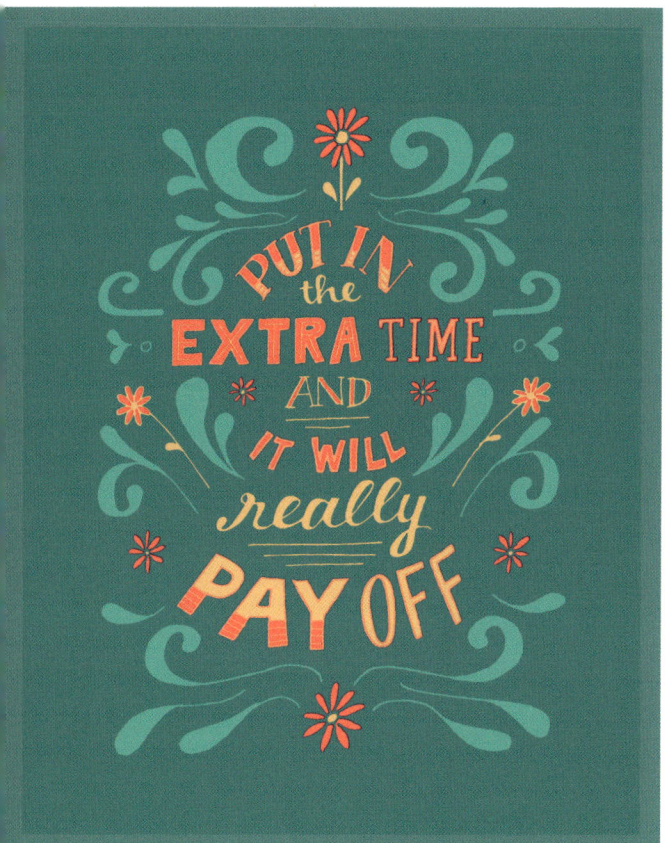

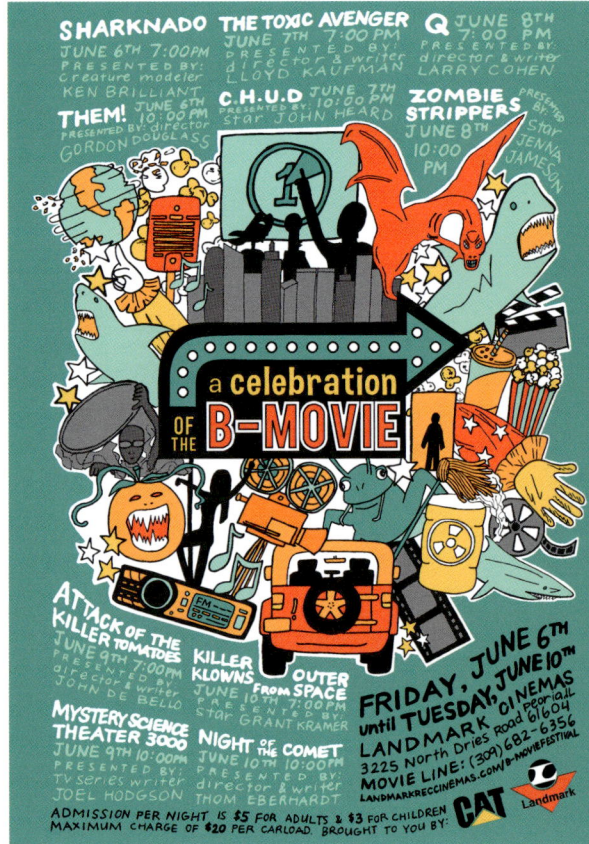

There are so many applications of hand lettering from package design to posters to shirts to special quotes.

Hand lettering can be an extremely unique and personal way to remember a loved one.

Tip: Challenge yourself to illustrate a single letter of the alphabet each day for 26 days. You can practice a variety of styles or create a cohesive alphabet. You can then turn your collection into printed materials like t-shirts.

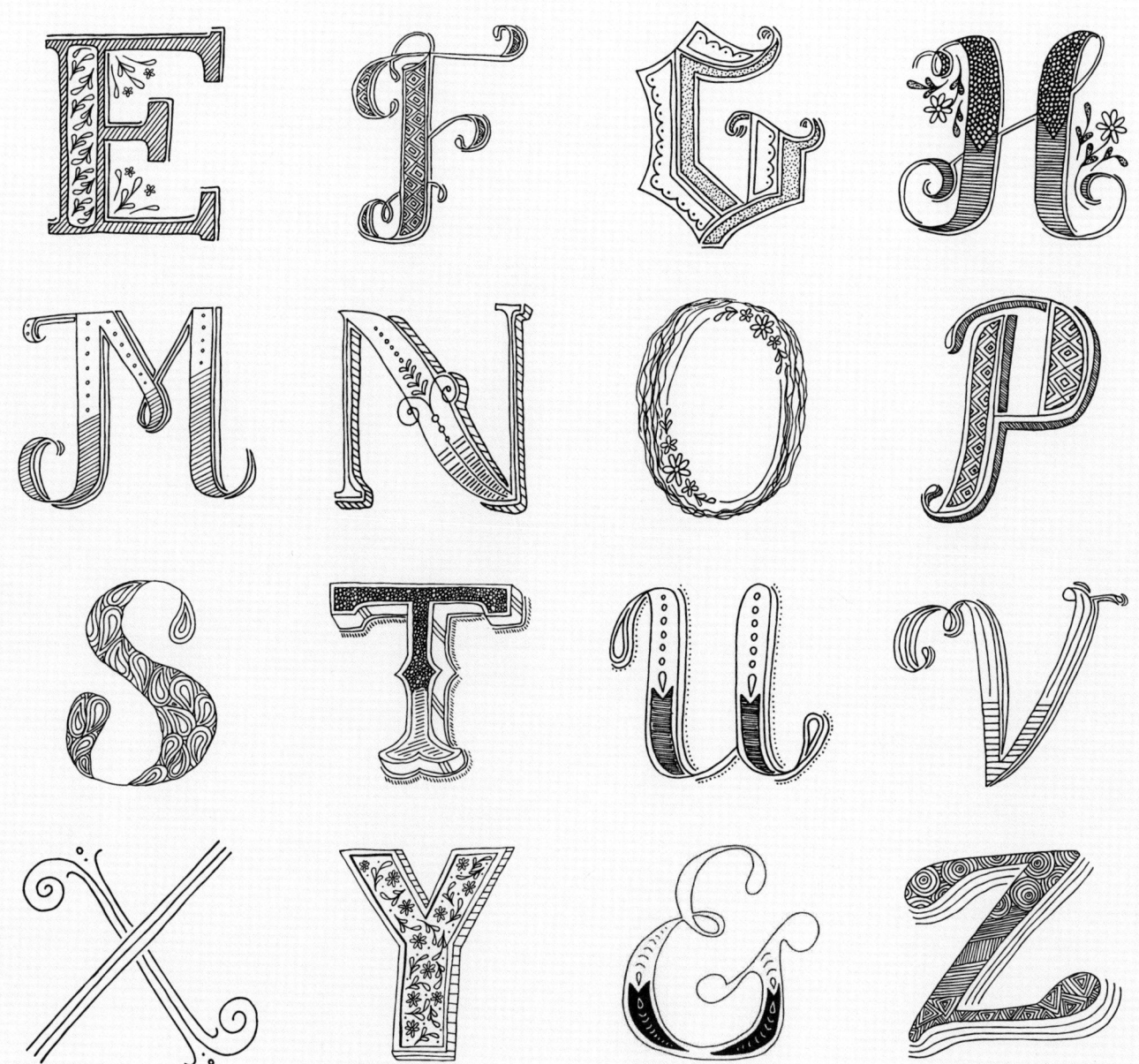

CHECK OUT THESE *GREAT* resources

Whatever You Are, Be a Good One: 100 Inspirational Quotations by Lisa Congdon. San Francisco: Chronicle LLC, 2014.

Drawing Type: An Introduction to Illustrating Letterforms by Alex Fowkes. Beverly, MA: Rockport, 2014.

Sharpie Art Workshop: Techniques & Ideas for Transforming Your World by Timothy Goodman. Beverly, MA: Rockport, 2015.

Little Book of Lettering by Emily Gregory. San Francisco, CA: Chronicle, 2012.

In Progress: See Inside a Lettering Artist's Sketchbook and Process, from Pencil to Vector by Jessica Hische. San Francisco, CA: Chronicle LLC, 2015.

Creative Lettering and Beyond: Inspiring Tips, Techniques, and Ideas for Hand-lettering Your Way to Beautiful Works of Art by Kirkendall, Gabri Joy, Laura Lavender, Julie Manwaring, and Shauna Lynn Panczyszyn. Irvine, CA: Walter Foster, 2014.

Thinking with Type: A Critical Guide for Designers, Writers, Editors, & Students (2nd Revised and Expanded Edition by Ellen Lupton. New York: Princeton Architectural, 2010.

Hand-Lettering Ledger by Mary Kate McDevitt. San Francisco, CA: Chronicle, 2014.

Hand Job: A Catalog of Type by Michael Perry. New York: Princeton Architectural, 2007.

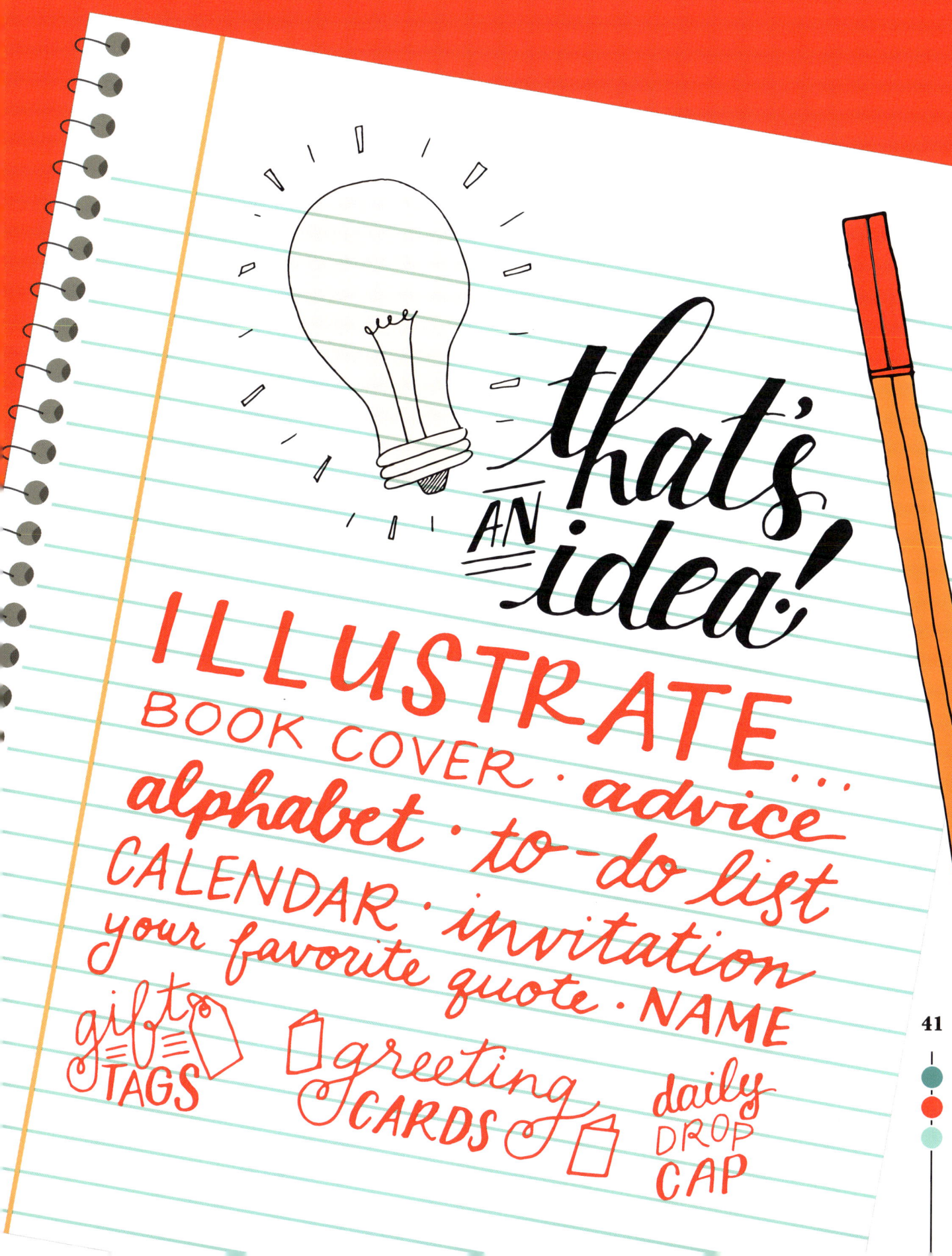